# Kings, Bishops, Knights, and Pawns

# Kings, Bishops, Knights, and Pawns

## *Life in a Feudal Society*

by Ralph Arnold

Illustrated by W. T. Mars

W · W · Norton & Company · Inc · New York

Published simultaneously in the Dominion of
Canada by George J. McLeod, Limited, Toronto

PRINTED IN THE UNITED STATES OF AMERICA
3 4 5 6 7 8 9 0

# Contents

# Kings, Bishops,
# Knights, and Pawns

# Chapter 1

# The Beginning

In the long-past period of history with which this book is concerned, most people lived very much from hand to mouth. They were accustomed to war, lawlessness, and violence. Justice was a hit-or-miss affair; and there were no national police forces. It was quite natural that the weak and defenseless should have turned to those who were stronger for help and protection; and that, in return, they should have been ready to pay for this help and protection in various ways.

It was through personal links or ties of this kind that feudalism, or the feudal system, began.

Today, the expression "a Feudal System" suggests either a brightly colored and romantic chessboard world in which Kings and Queens and Knights and Castles and Bishops and humble Pawns all played their parts; or else an old-fashioned and unfair system of government.

In practice, the feudal system provided a means — a method — of providing Kings with the well-armed and well-trained mounted soldiers that they needed for their armies. And it made certain that every subject of a King, great or small, powerful or weak, should have a lord to whom he owed obedi-

ence and respect and certain duties and services, but from whom he, in his turn, could claim protection and support and friendship.

Feudalism first started in the country between the rivers Loire and Rhine — the country which later became France — after the withdrawal of the Roman legions. The fall of the Roman Empire was followed by a period of war, confusion, and misery. The Frankish Kings — the Merovingian Kings as they are called — were faced with problems that they were quite unable to solve. Their territories were invaded. Their nobles were perpetually involved in blood feuds, which meant that they were more interested in fighting each other than in uniting to fight a common enemy. And a lack of money and of trustworthy and well-educated royal officials and of proper

10

roads and communications made it impossible for these Kings to govern properly or efficiently. As a result, many of their subjects who found themselves in need or in danger began to turn for help and protection to their richer and stronger neighbors.

## How the Feudal System Began

In the beginning, these feudal ties were entered into only between "free" men.

Men, in those days, were regarded as being either "free" or "unfree." Freedom stemmed from the independent ownership of land; and the sons of a free man were themselves free. A free man could expect to be called up to serve in the King's army, he was liable for payment of dues and taxes, and he had the right to go to one of the King's courts of justice to settle a dispute or to claim compensation for a wrong that someone else had done him. An unfree man was either a slave — in which case he would have no rights at all; or he was a peasant-serf. The few acres that peasant-serfs cultivated were provided by the landowners on whose estates they worked and to whom, for all practical purposes, they "belonged." An unfree peasant had to depend on his landlord for justice. He could not sell his holding, and he could not leave it without his landlord's permission. And in extreme cases he might even be bought or sold with his land like an ox or a cow.

The free men who formed links of their own free will with other free men during the reigns of the Merovingian Kings were generally younger sons who had inherited either no land at all or very little land, or who had been obliged to sell their land. Or they were adventurous men who enjoyed fighting —

12

and all free men then regarded themselves first and foremost as soldiers. If they were poor, because of their lack of land, they were afraid that without someone else's help they might be forced to become mere peasant-serfs. If they were adventurous, they knew that under the protection of a powerful baron they would have opportunities of showing their courage and skill as fighting men, and that they would have the chance of obtaining valuable loot and booty.

Such men "commended" themselves to their richer and more powerful neighbors, becoming the "vassals" of these "lords."

### The Ceremony of Homage

When a free man decided to become the vassal of a lord, the occasion was marked by a solemn ceremony. In those days hardly anyone except the clergy could read or write, and so ceremonies in which spoken vows were exchanged and in which gestures, and especially gestures with the hands, were used, had a very special importance.

First, the lord asked his vassal-to-be whether he wished, beyond any doubt, to become "his man." If the answer was "yes," the vassal-to-be knelt at his lord's feet, bareheaded and without his sword. Then the lord took his vassal's two hands between his own. That done, the agreement was sealed with a kiss.

This part of the ceremony — the voluntary surrender of one free man to another — was known as "homage."

Immediately after the ceremony of homage, the vassal, standing, swore an oath of obedience and faithfulness to his lord. This oath, known as the "oath of fealty," was spoken by the vassal, who held a Bible in his hands, or rested his hands

13

while he spoke on a casket that contained the bones of a saint.

"I promise by my faith," a vassal would say, "that from this time forward I will be faithful to ——— [naming his lord], and will maintain towards him my homage entirely against every man, in good faith and without any deception."

In another version of this same oath, the vassal would swear that he would be as faithful as a vassal should be to his lord, and that he would be "a friend to all his friends, and a foe to all his foes."

The ceremonies of homage and fealty were very personal and very deeply felt ceremonies; and the links which they forged were personal and deeply felt. They bore no resemblance whatever to the way in which a present-day employer might take someone into his service.

## The Oath of Fealty

The vassal promised to be faithful to his lord as long as they both lived; and undertook that he would serve, respect, obey, and advise him. But it was understood between them that he would be freed from his oath if his lord ordered him to do anything that was contrary to his rights as a free man. He would also be freed from his oath if his lord ordered him to do anything that was contrary to the allegiance which, as a free man, he owed to the King.

The lord, on his part, promised to protect his vassal, to come to his aid if he was attacked by an enemy, to stand by him in a court of law, to advise him, and to provide him with a proper maintenance — that is to say with food, drink, and a means of livelihood.

Both men knew that they must obey not only the letter but

14

also the spirit of the agreement. Failure on the part of either of them to "keep faith" was considered a serious crime, and was known as a "felony."

What services did a lord expect from his vassal, and what benefits did a vassal expect from his lord?

Generally a lord expected a vassal to be prepared to fight at his side and under his banner when he was called to arms by the King, or when he was engaged in a blood feud with a rival nobleman. The more vassals capable of fighting on horseback that a lord could call upon and rely on, the more powerful and important he would feel himself to be — and this was the chief reason why a lord welcomed vassals.

Apart from protection and friendship, the chief benefit that a vassal expected to receive from his lord was "maintenance." In the time of the Merovingian Kings, lords generally "maintained" their vassals by taking them into their own "halls" or houses, so that lords and their vassals lived together, the vassals being provided with free food and drink. It was also the custom for lords to provide their vassals with arms, armor, and horses; and, because the relationship was considered a personal one, and because they were looked on as being friends, vassals expected to be given presents by their lords from time to time, and to share in any spoils of war that might come their lords' way. Occasionally a lord would provide for a vassal by giving him a sum of money, or by granting him a small estate in return either for a very low rent, or for no rent at all. Such an estate was called a "benefice."


A Vassal and His Lord

Many years later, Bishop Fulbert of Chartres described the

15

duties of a vassal to his lord, and of a lord to his vassal, in these words:

He who swears fealty to his lord must always bear these six words in mind: "safe and sound," sure, honest, useful, easy, possible.

"Safe and sound," because he must never strike his lord in anger, or inflict any bodily injury upon him. Sure, because he must not injure his lord by betraying his secrets or his castles, upon which his lord's safety depends. Honest, because he must not injure his lord's interests or well-being by any trick or deceit. Useful, because he must be as careful of his lord's possessions as he would be of his own. Easy and possible, because he must not make it difficult for his lord to do anything that the latter may wish to do; and because he must not prevent his lord from doing something that his lord might otherwise be able to accomplish.

It is only right and proper that the vassal should refrain from injuring his lord in any of these ways. But he would not deserve the help and protection of his lord if he merely refrained from such harmful actions. It is not enough that a vassal should be careful never to injure his lord. He must actively help him. It is therefore essential, in the matter of the six duties that have been described, that the vassal, if he wishes to appear worthy of his lord's protection, should faithfully and to the best of his ability give his lord his advice and support, and that he should faithfully carry out the terms of the oath of fealty that he has sworn.

In the same way the lord must deal faithfully in all things with the vassal who has sworn fealty to him. If the lord fails in this duty, he will rightly be accused of bad faith, just as a vassal who is found to have failed in his duties to his lord is guilty of dishonesty and of a serious crime. . . .

This gives a good idea of what the link from which the feudal system started was like.

## Charlemagne's Mounted Soldiers

The Merovingian Kings were followed by the Carolingian Kings and Emperors, the most famous being the Emperor Charlemagne (771–814).

16

Charlemagne, in building up his great Empire, found that the national army, in which all free men had to serve, was slow, clumsy, and inefficient. The Franks had learnt many useful lessons from the invaders of Western Europe; among these lessons had been the use of stirrups, and the practice of shoeing horses. It seems extraordinary that neither the Greeks nor the Romans had discovered such an obvious aid to horsemanship as the stirrup; but it is a fact that the Franks copied the use of stirrups from the invaders who came from the Asian steppes, skilled horsemen who were also accustomed to shoe their horses with iron horseshoes.

These discoveries made mounted soldiers much more valuable in fighting than foot soldiers, because a soldier on a properly shod horse could reach the scene of the fighting quickly and, once in action with his feet firmly in the stirrups, he could use a lance effectively and could not easily be knocked off his mount.

The trouble was that only a rich man, or a man with a rich lord, could afford the arms and equipment that a mounted soldier needed.

The requirements of a mounted soldier were as follows: a war horse, which cost as much as six cows; a thick leather coat or jerkin, padded on the inside and sewn on the outside with plates or rings of metal, which was as expensive as his horse; a conical-shaped metal helmet with a projecting flap, called a "nasal," which protected his nose and part of his face (a helmet like this cost as much as three cows); a shield, generally made of lime wood covered with toughened leather; a sword; and a lance. The use of stirrups made it possible for mounted soldiers to employ long lances. In the charge, the lance was held under the rider's armpit; and its weight, when at rest, was taken by the stirrup.

# Feudalism Becomes the Fashion

Apart from the members of Charlemagne's own royal body-guard, whose horses and arms and equipment he supplied

himself, the only available soldiers who were trained and equipped to fight on horseback were the nobles and their vassals. But the Emperor found that the loyalty of these subjects was sometimes in doubt, and so he hit on the plan of persuading his nobles to become his own vassals, rewarding them with additional estates. In this way the nobles were bound to the Emperor by the ceremony of homage and by the oath of fealty. Because they had been given additional estates, they were able to enlist more fighting vassals of their own. And because the Emperor's policy had made vassalage fashionable, not only poor men but also rich men began "commending" themselves to men richer and more powerful than themselves.

Another important step towards the wider acceptance of a feudal system was also taken at this time. Like his predecessors, Charlemagne found it difficult to govern his Empire efficiently; and so he decided to make use of the feudal arrangement of vassalage to help his officials to carry out their duties. His object was to make certain that every free man should have a lord. The lord would then be held responsible for "his man's" protection and well-being, and he would also have to see that his vassal performed his service in the national army, paid his national taxes and dues, and attended a royal court of justice when his presence there was required.

## Knights' Fiefs

The break-up of Charlemagne's Empire, which resulted in the birth of the separate states of France, Burgundy, Germany, and Italy, was brought about by the invasion of Western Europe by Saracens, or Arabs, from the south; by Hungarian Magyars from the east; and by Scandinavians, or Vikings, from the north. In the course of half a century of bloodshed and confusion, feudal arrangements struck a firm root —but the results were very different from those which the Emperor Charlemagne had intended when he had made feudalism "official." Powerful nobles took more and more vassals into their service, built themselves castles and strongholds, and, forgetting their oaths of fealty, often set themselves up as local tyrants and defied royal authority.

By the year A.D. 850, which is when the feudal system in Western Europe can be said to have begun in real earnest, feudal arrangements in the territory between the river Loire and the river Rhine had become established along certain well-understood lines, and had come to play an all-important part not only in the lives of the King and his nobles and their vassals but also in the lives of the peasant-serfs.

It had, by this time, become the general rule that the service that a vassal owed to his lord in return for protection and maintenance was military service — as a mounted soldier. And the vassals of barons began to be called "chevaliers," or "knights."

It had also become the rule rather than the exception that a lord should provide his vassals with a means of livelihood not by taking them into his own household, but by granting them estates. Such estates were called "knights' fiefs," and a vassal who held a knight's fief was thought of as being in a position to maintain himself, and to provide his own arms, armor, and horses. At first, vassals were granted such estates only for their lifetimes. When they died, or if they failed to carry out their vassals' duties properly, the estates went back to their lords. But the custom soon grew up that such estates could be passed on from fathers to sons, the sons inheriting, of course, their fathers' responsibilities for military service.

Even bishops and abbots, because they were great landowners, often had to pay homage and swear oaths of fealty to the King, and all churchmen who held great estates had to render services — sometimes in the shape of prayers for the health of the King's soul, or for the health of the souls of the barons who had given them their estates, and sometimes in the shape of providing knights to serve in the King's army.

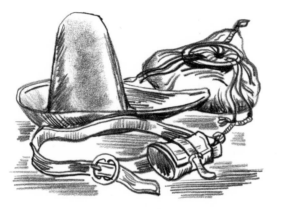

All the great royal officals were vassals of the King, and were given grants of land in return for their services instead of salaries. The lesser servants of the royal household — the great army of cooks and tailors and falconers and huntsmen — were also given small estates instead of being paid wages in money.

And finally it had become the custom that the unfree peasant-serfs who were responsible for cultivating all these country estates should go through a simpler ceremony of

21

swearing oaths of fealty to their landlords. They, too, promised to respect, obey, and be faithful to their lords; but the services that they undertook to perform in return for the few acres of land they held and for their lords' promises of protection and maintenance were not, of course, promises of military service. They were promises to work with their own hands on their private lords' estates.

So it can be seen that the network of feudal links had come to cover all classes of men; and that, in these links, the idea of services owned in return for grants of land was becoming increasingly important.

The importance that the granting of land played in the feudal scheme of things was emphasized by a ceremony. When anyone, from a great noble to a peasant-serf, was "invested" with a holding of land, the man who was granting the land handed to the man to whom it was being granted a stick or a stalk of corn or a clod of earth. If an estate was being given to a knight, the knight would be handed a lance. A noble, who already had vassals of his own, would be handed a banner. These various objects were regarded as representing the land that was passing from one man to another.

A Profession Fit for a Gentleman

What were these French barons and knights like, and what kind of lives did they lead?

Though they did no work, and lived on the produce of their estates which were cultivated by their peasant-serfs, they were rich by the standards of those times; and fighting was the be-all and end-all of their existences, the pride and purpose of their lives. Of all class of men in a feudal society, the most admired, respected, and envied were the men who had been trained to fight on horseback.

These feudal aristocrats must be pictured as rough and uncouth, unable to read or write, physically immensely strong, and skilled only in the art and practice of war, in hunting, and in the tactics of the tournament and joust.

Hunting, when there was no fighting going on, played a large part in their lives. A great deal of land was then still uncultivated; there were endless miles of wild woodland and forest; and deer and wild boar were hunted with packs of hounds, hares were coursed with greyhounds, and smaller game and birds were flown at and killed by falcons. Hunting was regarded not only as a sport, but as a method of keeping down wild animals which could do a great deal of damage to the standing crops, and also as a method of providing households with much-needed meat. The sheep and cattle were generally miserably thin, and there was not enough foodstuff available to keep all of them alive through the winter months. The meat from the beasts which had to be slaughtered each November was salted and kept in barrels, where it often went bad.

Tournaments, like much else in a feudal society, began in France — as dress-rehearsals, or practices, for actual fighting. They were really "battle games," in which, on Saints' Days or other great occasions, teams of knights fought each other in what was called a mêlée. There were no rules, goals, or boundaries; it was a dangerous and bloody sport. Later on, elaborate rules were drawn up for tournaments; and jousts, or single-combat encounters, became popular.

Although all barons and nearly all knights were landowners, they took little or no interest in the management of their estates, which were looked after by their stewards. They were in no sense "gentlemen farmers" or "country gentlemen" as

23

these terms are understood today. Then it was considered that fighting was the only profession fit for a gentleman. It is known from contemporary stories and songs that these barons and knights suffered badly from boredom — which is scarcely surprising; that they had enormous appetites; that they had an astonishing disregard for danger and for death; that they were moody, and subject to fits of uncontrolled anger; that they could be, and often were, horribly cruel; and that, at the same time, they were generally deeply religious, experiencing spells of genuine remorse and of black despair.

At least some part of their reckless courage and of their disregard for their own and for other people's lives came from a belief that life on this earth was much less important than the life to come. They were also convinced that the end of the

25

world was close at hand. For a long time it was expected that the Day of Judgement would happen during the year A.D. 1000 — which was always referred to as the "Day of Wrath." Although they were Christians, they were very superstitious, believing in demons and spirits.

Since fighting was to be their profession, the sons of barons and knights were taken away from their mothers when they were seven years old and, instead of being sent to school, were placed in the households of other barons and knights. First they were taught the rough-and-ready manners of the times. They served their elders and betters at table; they carved the meat and placed the helpings on the slices of three-day-old bread which served as plates; they poured out the wine into horn cups; and, after a meal, they took around the basins of water in which the company rinsed their fingers — a necessary custom before forks were used. They were taught the art of hunting in all its different branches. And they were taught how to ride, and how to fight on horseback. They were also expected to "squire," or accompany, their lords wherever they went.

## Dubbing a Knight

When one of these young squires had completed his training, he was "dubbed" a knight. In the course of this ceremony an older knight handed the knight-to-be his arms and armor, fastening a sword round the young man's waist and then giving him a hard slap on the neck or chest with the flat of his hand. This, it was said, was the only blow that a knight might never return. The new knight then jumped on to his horse, and gave a display of riding and of tilting at a "quintain" — a barrel or something of that kind suspended from a pole.

## Life in the First Castles

Barons and knights lived in houses that could be defended against attacks by their enemies.

A baron living on one of his estates in the country would own a wooden hall or house defended by a stout palisade fence made of logs of wood set upright, fronted by a deep ditch.

His house would be bigger, but in other ways not much more elaborate, than the other wooden houses in the village that were lived in by his peasant-serfs. It would have a single high-raftered room, like a present-day farmer's barn, in which the baron and his wife and children; any vassal knights who might be living with him and any young men training to be knights; his men-at-arms, and his numerous servants would all eat their meals and spend such of the time as they were indoors. Generally this single big hall was on the ground floor, but sometimes it was raised up above a store-room, and then it was reached by an outside stairway or ladder. There might be another smaller room leading out of the hall — the "bower," in which the baron and his wife retired each evening to sleep; but quite often the bower was a detached room or shed in the yard behind the house.

There would be trestle tables on the beaten-earth floor of the baron's hall, backless wooden benches to sit on, a sideboard on which any silver that he owned was displayed, and a few roughly made wooden cupboards and stools. There would probably be only one bed in the house. Sacks stuffed with hay or straw, thrown down on the floor and covered by skins or woolen blankets, served the rest of the household. If a baron was rich, when a feast was held in his hall to celebrate a Saint's Day or the presence of guests or the occasion of a marriage or some other family festivity, tapestries would be brought out to cover the smoke-grimed walls — the room would be heated by an open fire burning in a scooped-out hollow of the floor. There would be no chimney, and the smoke would have to find its way out through the small, high, glassless windows that were fitted with wooden shutters. On the occasion of a feast, there would be a vast amount of eating and drinking, and the company would be amused by strolling minstrels — professional entertainers who recited stories about heroes and battles, sang songs, and played on musical instruments.

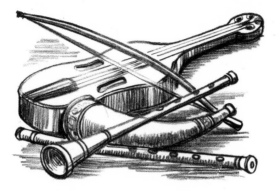

The kitchen would be in the enclosed yard at the back of the house — kitchens were usually placed well away from the houses they served because, since all the buildings were then made of wood, there was a very real danger of fire. The stables for the horses would also be in this yard, together with barns, a dovecote, and a belfry.

The church, which the baron would have built for his village, was generally close to his house.

A rich and powerful baron might sometimes have built himself a castle; but castles, at this time, were very different from the popular present-day idea of a medieval castle. They were simply wooden towers, into which their owners and their families and their households could retire in times of danger.

These towers had always been defended as strongly as possible with palisade fences and ditches; but in France a new form of castle-building was invented. A huge mound of earth was piled up to a height of some fifty feet, with a circumference at its rounded flattened summit of about seventy-five feet; and the wooden "castle" was perched on the top of this mound.

The advantage of this new type of castle was that it could be defended more efficiently against attackers. A deep ditch was dug around the base of the mound, and a strong palisade fence ringed its summit. The lower story of the tower itself was generally used as a store-room, the living-room being on the first floor. From the top of the tower, a watchman could see an enemy approaching from a very long way off.

As a house to live in, a castle of this kind had many disadvantages. The only method of getting into it was by a bridge that crossed the ditch at the base of the mound, and then by a wooden staircase or ladder that ran up the side of the mound to the gate in the palisade fence. After that, in order to reach the living-room it was necessary to climb another ladder inside the tower itself. On the other hand, these disadvantages also faced any enemy who was trying to get inside the castle, and the fact that the tower was raised up on a mound made it more difficult for anyone to set it on fire.

A baron who owned one of these towers usually lived in a hall, or house, built in an oblong-shaped enclosure at the foot of the mound. This enclosure was also surrounded with a ditch and a palisade fence. If the castle was attacked, the baron and his household would retire into the tower, while his peasant-serfs and the sheep and cattle would take refuge inside the enclosure. Very often the side of the castle mound that was farthest away from the enclosure would be defended by some natural obstacle like a river or a stream, or the steep side of a valley.

A knight's house would be just like a baron's house, though on a rather smaller scale.

To a present-day reader the strangest thing about this way of life may be the fact that even the head of the house and his wife enjoyed practically no privacy. The hall, which was their

only living-room — and sometimes their bedroom as well — must always have been filled, day and night, with children and soldiers and servants. Privacy was something that people did not bother about in those days.

Time was another thing that they did not bother about. Water-clocks — the only form of mechanical clock that had been invented — were rare and expensive objects; hour-glasses were very little used; and sundials were unreliable. So most people got up with the dawn, and went to bed when the sun set.

Women in these times must have led hard and uncomfortable lives. Stories and poems written at the time suggest that the wives of barons and knights often ruled their households and their young children and even their estates when their husbands were away at war, with great firmness; but they also suggest that most barons and knights married not for love but in order to obtain more land or more money. The romantic and chivalrous treatment of women had not yet come to be thought of as among the first duties of a knight.

This, briefly, is how and why feudal arrangements began in the country between the Loire and the Rhine; how these links worked; and what one small but important class of the people who made up a feudal society was like, and how its members lived.

The feudal system, spreading from France, took root firmly and quickly in Burgundy and Italy, and more slowly in Germany and in England. Feudalism, however, in a very complete form was brought to England by Duke William of Normandy, who was himself a vassal of the King of France.

Life in England, from the Norman Conquest until the year 1250, is the best example of what life in a feudal society was like.

# Chapter 2

# The Middle

In the year 1066, Duke William of Normandy, with a feudal army of some six thousand mounted barons and knights and about the same number of foot soldiers, defeated King Harold and his bodyguard and the Sussex contingent of the English national army at the battle of Hastings.

Duke William was the remarkable ruler of a remarkable people. The Normans were descended from Vikings, or Northmen. These Northmen, having successfully invaded France and having occupied the territory that came to be called Normandy, had been converted to the Christian faith, had adopted the French language, and had copied the French feudal customs of homage and fealty, fighting on horseback, and the building of castles.

As soon as he had been crowned King in London, William the Conqueror set about establishing a chain of feudal links which connected all the different classes of men in English society.

Faced with the question "To what extent could English society before the Norman Conquest have been described as feudal?" historians have given very different answers.

Five hundred years earlier, the Anglo-Saxons, after invading Britain, and driving the Britons into the extreme west and north of the island, had settled down as farmers; and England had become a land of small agricultural villages. In these villages, each free man had held and farmed his share of the land, which was thought of as belonging to his village — or rather to the village family group, or clan, to which he belonged. Originally, all the free men in any Anglo-Saxon village may, in fact, have been related to each other; and although in course of time this had ceased to be the case, these family groups had gone on playing an important part in the lives of their members.

## Anglo-Saxon Farmers

But a present-day farmer would be amazed if he suddenly found himself standing in one of these Anglo-Saxon farmers' shoes.

As a start, he would be astonished to find that his farm, instead of being a block of land divided up into large or small fenced or hedged-in fields, consisted of some sixty half-acre strips scattered about haphazardly in each of his village's three great cultivated fields; and he would also be astonished to find that his strips were not fenced around, and were separated from the strips belonging to all the other farmers in his village only by open furrows.

Then he would be amazed to find that while he was responsible for cultivating his own strips, he was allowed no choice in the matter of what crops he could grow on them. The village council, of which he might be a member, would decide each year which of the three village fields should remain uncultivated, or "lie fallow," for the next twelve months, so that its soil could have a rest; and this same council would also decide what crops should be grown by all the strip-holders in each of the other two fields, when all the strips should be plowed, when the crops should be sown, when the fields should be harrowed, and when the crops should be harvested.

And finally he would be surprised and worried to discover that his farmhouse and his farm buildings were situated in the village street, quite a long way from his strips; that except for a small paddock adjoining his house, he had no meadowland of his own in which his sheep and his other beasts could be turned out to graze; and that instead, he had the right, along with all the other farmers in his village, to send his plow-oxen and his cows and his sheep to graze on the village common pasture, and that at certain times of the year his farm stock could also graze on the fallow field, in the village hay-meadow, and in the stubble fields after the harvest had been reaped. He could send his pigs, along with all the other farmers' pigs, to root for acorns and beech mast in the village woodland; and he would find that each summer he would be allotted a strip of the village hay-meadow, from which he would have to make enough hay to keep at least some of his beasts alive through the winter months.

It would have to be explained to the puzzled twentieth-century farmer that this was called the "open-field" system of farming — because each of the three great village fields was fenced around only when a crop was growing in it; that few, if any, of the village farmers could afford to own as many as the eight oxen which were needed to pull one of the heavy plows of those days; that four farmers generally had to club together and pool their oxen in order to plow their strips; and that this elaborate system of pooling and sharing — common pasture land, shares in a common hay-meadow, common grazing rights, and a planned system of sowing and harvesting crops — was probably the only system that could be devised by which these smallholding farmers, with their limited land and implements and money, could ever have grown enough grain and maintained enough sheep and cattle and pigs to support themselves and their families through the twelve months of every year.

## Feudal Beginnings in England

All this may sound as if English society, before the Norman Conquest, was a society in which all men were equal; and in which all the available land in the country was shared out among them equally.

But this was not the case. At one end of the social scale were the Kings, who owned a great deal of land; and immediately below them came the earls and thanes, as the English nobles were called, who also owned considerable estates, as did the bishops and abbots to whom the Kings and great nobles had granted large properties. And at the other end of the social scale, below the village farmers, there were still a few slaves, and a good many peasant-serfs who, in every village, had been given tiny cottages to live in. These peasants had also been provided with small plots of land which they cultivated; in return for these plots, they were expected to work for several days each week all through the year for the thane or the abbot or the farmer from whom they held their land.

When, from about the year 800 onwards, the Vikings had invaded England, the English Kings had not been strong enough to give their poorer and weaker subjects proper protection, and new links had been forged between many of the free village farmers and the thanes, or nobles, who lived in their villages.

These links had been of the same kind as the links that had been forged, two or three hundred years before, between Frankish free men and their richer and more powerful neighbors. Individual free Anglo-Saxon village farmers, in the misery and confusion caused by the Viking invasions, had of their own free wills "commended" themselves to, and had sought protection from, the better-armed and more powerful thanes.

Then, in his efforts to prevent the Vikings overrunning the whole of England, King Alfred (871–99) had found that the thanes, who though they did not fight on horseback nevertheless owned horses and armor and weapons and were able to ride to the scene of a battle, were more effective as soldiers than the slow-moving foot soldiers of the national army, in which all free men had the duty to serve; and so he had copied Charlemagne's earlier example, and had given promising soldiers estates which would enable them to buy arms, armor, and horses.

The difference between these links and the links that had been widely established in France was that in England the services that the King demanded from his thanes in return for the estates that he had given them, and the services that the thanes demanded from the village farmers for the protection that they had promised them, were less definite. They depended on "understandings" rather than on cut-and-dried promises. This was especially true of the links that existed between the village farmers and the thanes. Grants of land, by way of "maintenance," formed no part of these agreements, because most of the farmers already had land of their own. A thane's protection was usually paid for by annual payments in money or in produce, and by occasional presents.

## The Norman Conquest

But once one class of men in any society has begun to depend in any way on another class, this dependence is likely to grow stronger with time, rather than weaker. By the year 1066, copying the feudal arrangements that had grown up in France, English earls and the greater thanes had begun to pay homage and to swear oaths of fealty to the King. And lesser thanes had become the vassals of earls. It had been laid down by the King that every free man must have a lord, and many of the poorer free village farmers who were unable to pay rents or had fallen on bad times had found themselves doing several days' work each week on their lords' home farms.

So it would probably be true to say that English society, at the time of the Norman Conquest, was at least partly feudal.

The conqueror of a country is able to enforce what arrangement he chooses on the society of that country; and the arrangements that he will enforce will be the arrangements which will best suit his own purposes.

The feudal system that William the Conqueror imposed on

English society was firmly and squarely based on grants of land.

Every single acre of land in England, William declared, belonged to the King of England. It was his to do what he liked with; while he kept many English estates for himself, he granted huge but scattered properties all over the country to the Norman barons and knights who had taken an active part in the Conquest; and, because he was a strong supporter of the Church, he also gave a great deal of English land to Norman bishops and abbots. This meant, of course, that the English earls and thanes and the village farmers had their lands taken away from them — which is the usual fate of landowners in a conquered country.

## Knights for the King's Army

King William had two objects in mind when he made these grants of land to his fellow-Normans. In the first place he was keeping the promises that he had made to these nobles, who would never have crossed the Channel with him if they had not expected rich rewards. And in the second place he saw in these grants of land a method of making certain that he would have enough well-trained and well-armed mounted soldiers to serve in his army.

In return for their new English estates, the Norman nobles and bishops and abbots had to pay homage and swear oaths of fealty to the King; and each had to undertake that he would produce, when he was called upon to do so, a fixed number of properly trained and properly equipped knights for the King's service. The number of knights for which each vassal, or tenant-in-chief, of the King was responsible depended upon the size of his estates; and it was understood that if a tenant-in-chief failed in his duties, his estates would be taken away from him.


## Land in Return for Services Rendered

No hard and fast rules were laid down as to how the tenants-in-chief were to "maintain" the knights for whom they were responsible. They could, if they liked, house and feed them and provide them with their equipment; but in most cases tenants-in-chief granted their knights estates of their own — knights' fiefs or, as they came to be called in England, knights' fees. In return for the grant of such an estate, which would provide him with a livelihood and the means to buy and maintain his arms, his armor and his horse, a knight had to pay homage and swear an oath of fealty to his lord; and he had to undertake to serve at his lord's side and under his lord's banner whenever his lord received a call to the King's service.

A Norman knight had to promise other services to his lord. He had to undertake garrison duty in his lord's castle for so many days in each year. When they were together, he had to hold the stirrup when his lord mounted his horse, and on ceremonial occasions he was expected to ride at his lord's side. And, by feudal custom, he was expected to give his lord a sum of money when the lord's eldest daughter was married, when the lord's eldest son was made a knight, and when a ransom was demanded if the lord had been taken prisoner. These money payments, which were supposed to be friendly acts performed at important, or critical, times in the lord's life, were known as "feudal aids."

Both the King and his tenants-in-chief granted estates to people in return for services other than turning out to fight

on horseback.

The King did not pay the officials and servants of his enormous household salaries or wages in money. Instead, he granted them estates. The great officials ranked as royal vassals; the lesser officials as knights; and the servants ranked as "sergeants." One of King William's successors granted an estate in Kent to a servant called Salamon de Campis in return for the service of holding the King's head if he suffered from seasickness when he crossed the Channel from Dover to France. The great barons paid their retainers and servants in the same way. Land was a great deal more plentiful than money.

Out of their enormous holdings of land, the King and his tenants-in-chief kept only a few large village farms, or manors as they were now called, for their own personal use. At first it was their custom to spend the year traveling around from one manor to another. In the course of these visits, they and their households would eat up all the food that had been produced on these manors and stored away in barns. Produce from the manors that belonged to bishops and abbots was regularly sent in carts to the residences of the bishops, and to the monasteries over which the abbots ruled.

An estate was only valuable if it was properly cultivated; the problem that faced the owners of all these estates was to make certain that there should always be enough farmers and peasants to plow their lands and to sow and harvest their crops. Under the feudal system, as organized in England by William the Conqueror, this problem was easily solved.

Before the Norman Conquest, while the King and the Anglo-Saxon thanes and the Anglo-Saxon bishops and abbots had owned large estates, a great deal of the land in England had been owned and farmed by village farmers. At one fell swoop, all the holdings of these village farmers had been taken away from them because, under the new feudal scheme of things, all the land in England without exception was held to belong to the King, and because the King had granted most of it to his tenants-in-chief who, in their turn, had granted estates to their knights. But the last thing that these new landowners desired was that the former owners — the village farmers — should stop cultivating their strips in the village fields. If they did, all these fields would quickly become overgrown with weeds, and would produce no crops.

## The New Norman Lords

So it was taken for granted that the village farmers, instead of owning their strips, were now to think of themselves as the tenants of the Normans who were the new owners of the villages, or manors, in which they lived; in return for the right of being allowed to go on farming their strips in their village open fields, which was their only means of livelihood, these village farmers had to undertake to perform certain services for their new lords.

At first sight, this may sound like a very sweeping and revolutionary change. But it has to be remembered that, by the year 1066, most if not all of the Anglo-Saxon village farmers had already been linked in much the same way with the thanes, to whom they or their fathers or grandfathers had "commended" themselves.

A change that must have seemed much more dramatic was the change of lords. The thanes, to whom they were accustomed, had disappeared; and in their places were new Norman lords of the manor with whom, because these Norman landowners spoke only French, the villagers were unable to exchange a single word.

But here again, though they must have wondered how their new lords would treat them, the villagers can have had no great cause for alarm. In most cases, the same men as before were employed actually to look after the estates of these new lords. The same village councils went on meeting in the same way in order to decide how the village fields should be cultivated. The free farmers could still go to a royal court of justice; and while the peasant-serfs had to depend on new lords for justice, the manor courts which they attended were managed in just the same way as the courts to which they had been accustomed. And, most importantly of all, the village farmers and the peasants continued to cultivate the same strips and plots in the same open fields in exactly the same way as before.

Except for the fact that a good many formerly free village farmers slid down the social scale and became unfree peasants, the Norman Conquest made less actual difference to the village farmers and peasants, who then formed the great majority of the population of England, than to any other class of people in English society.

It is often said that a feudal society was made up of men who prayed, men who fought, and men who labored.

Some account has already been given in this book of the men who fought — the French barons and knights who lived between the years 850 and 1066.

The barons and knights in Norman England had very much the same outlook as these French barons and knights, and lived very much the same sort of lives; and they brought one new feudal custom with them across the Channel.

## Motte-and-Bailey Castles

Before the Norman Conquest, there had been no castles in England. The first thing that William the Conqueror and his barons did after the battle of Hastings was to build dozens of castles — motte-and-bailey castles as they were called — which were designed to show the conquered English, both in the towns and in the countryside, that the Normans were their masters. These castles were wooden towers, built in the French style, the "mottes" being the mounds of earth on which the towers were perched, and the "baileys" the enclosed courtyards at the foot of the mounds.

In a few cases the towers, instead of being made of wood, were made of stone. This marked the first beginnings of stone medieval castles.

## The Men Who Prayed

Religion played a very large part in the ordinary everyday lives of people in a feudal society. For everyone, death — death from violence, death from disease, or death from famine — seemed just round the corner, and it is not surprising that people often regarded life on this earth as a time of misery that had to be endured before a better and happier life could be enjoyed, or that God was thought of as being close at hand, overseeing everything that men did.

For these reasons the clergy, and especially the monks, through whose prayers men believed that they could be assured of going to Heaven when they died, were regarded with great reverence and awe.

This may sound as if everyone in a feudal society was always miserable, and that people, then, never enjoyed themselves. Of course this was not the case. But it would probably be true to say that just as people in a feudal society were accustomed to having a lord to whom they looked for protection and to whom, in return, they were prepared to render services, so, in those days, people looked to God for protection, and willingly performed the services of going to church, and giving a tenth of all their goods and of all the produce of their farms to the clergy, who were God's servants. For the same reason, Kings and rich men gladly gave lands to bishops and to the abbots of monasteries, generally asking that, in return, the priests should say special prayers for the health of their souls.

Religion even played its part in courts of law. In those days, if a crime was committed in a village, it was the duty of the men chosen to represent the village to go to the local royal court of justice and produce, or "present," the man whom they suspected of having committed the crime. If the accused man and the representatives of the village to which he belonged denied this charge, and protested that he was innocent, it was sometimes left to God to decide whether he was guilty or not.

46

The accused man would be thrown into the water, or he would be given a red-hot bar of iron to hold. If he failed to sink, or if after three days his fingers had festered, it was believed that, by "the judgement of God," he must be guilty.

"The men who prayed" in a feudal society, whether they were English or French or German or Italian by birth, all belonged to the same Church — the Church of Rome. Western

Europe, was then often called "Christendom"; and the strongest link that bound the different European countries together was the fact that the bishops and abbots and the monks and the village priests everywhere all owed obedience to the Pope, who was the Bishop of Rome.

Lanfranc, whom William the Conqueror made Archbishop of Canterbury, was born and educated in Pavia, in northern Italy. Then he was made abbot, or head, of the monastery at Caen, in Normandy. After that he came to Canterbury to be leader of the Church in England. That is something that could never happen today. And, in addition to belonging, so to speak, to one great family, all the clergy except a few of the less well-educated village priests could speak Latin — so they had a common language.

Of all the men who prayed in a feudal society, the most admired and respected were the monks, who of their own free wills had cut themselves off from the ordinary life of the world and who, year in and year out, performed a daily round of services in the churches attached to the monasteries in which they lived as a community, or family, bound by very strict rules. Both in England and in the other countries of Christendom most of the monasteries followed the rules laid down by St. Benedict of Nursia, who had died in the year A.D. 550. These Benedictine monks were known as "the black monks," because of the color of the habits that they wore.

The life of a Benedictine monk sounds very hard and very monotonous; but it is the life that is still led by many monks today.

# Life in a Monastery

Their day began at midnight, when the monks were summoned from the dormitory in which they slept to the service of Matins in their church. Generally there was a covered passageway leading direct from the dormitory to the church. The service of Laud followed at 1 a.m. During these early morning services, one monk used to go round with a lantern, shining it in the eyes of each sleepy worshiper. Any monk who had been caught dozing off was obliged himself to take the lantern, and to continue the round of inspection. After Laud, the monks went back to their beds, to be roused again at 7 a.m. to take part in the daybreak service of Prime. After Prime, all the members of the monastic "family" washed, and the young boys who lived in the monastery and any especially old or infirm monks were allowed to break their fast with a meal, eaten standing up, of bread and the third of a pint of wine.

The next church service, Tierce or Morrow Mass, was followed by a meeting when the business affairs of the monastery

were discussed — and it must be remembered that all monasteries owned great estates.

This meeting over, the younger monks and the boys who had been sent to the monastery by their parents to receive their education, had a precious hour when they could play games while their elders rested or slept. Bowls was a favorite pastime, and so was checkers. The monasteries, then, were the only schools in the country, and the boys who attended the monastery schools went as small children, and stayed until they grew up.

High Mass was celebrated at noon; and at 2.30 or 3 p.m. came dinner in the hall — which, except during the summer months, was the only meal of the day. In monasteries where the rules were strictly kept, the monks would be given only a pound of bread each, and two kinds of vegetables. In less strict monasteries fish, vegetables, pastry, poultry, cheese, wine, and milk were provided. The rest of the afternoon was spent in work or in study.


## Before Printing Was Invented

The clergy were the only people, except for Kings and a few of the nobles, who could read and write. Before the invention of printing, it was the monks who copied and bound the scriptures and other books; they were skilled "illuminators," drawing and coloring the splendid illustrations and initial letters which are the glory of medieval manuscripts· And they were almost the only recorders of the events of the day. Very little would be known about the history of feudal times if it had not been for the work of these monkish chroniclers.

In a monastery, all the writing and studying was done in the

covered passageways or cloisters which ran around the inside of the main quadrangle. The church formed the north side of this quadrangle; the refectory hall was on its south side; the monks' dormitory was on its east side; and on its west side were the rooms set aside for guests.

Since there were few inns or hotels, travelers as a matter of course sought food and shelter in monasteries, where anyone was allowed to stay, free of charge, for two nights. People traveled about a great deal in those days — noblemen visited their different estates, merchants went from town to town, and all classes of men made pilgrimages to visit the shrines and tombs of famous saints.

The service of Vespers was held in the church at 6 p.m., and between Easter and September 13, when the monks were permitted a second meal, Vespers was followed, if it was not a fast day, by a light supper of bread and cheese or fruit. During meals, the monks were not allowed to talk to one another, but instead listened to one of the community who read out loud from the Scriptures.

At 7 p.m. came the service of Compline. This service, like all the others, was announced by the ringing of the monastery bells. Half an hour later the monks went to their beds. At midnight the bells rang again, and the daily round began once more.

## Good and Bad Monks

Many of the monks in a feudal society were deeply religious and scholarly men who had chosen this hard way of life so as to serve God and their fellow men. As the monasteries grew richer through the gifts of land that were made to them, their rules were sometimes slackly administered, and some monks became lazy and greedy. Not all monasteries followed the original rules laid down by St. Benedict. The Cluniac monks followed a revised form of the Benedictine rules; and the Cistercian monks — the white monks — followed a still stricter form of these rules.

The Cistercian monks, in England, always chose very wild and deserted sites for their monasteries. They did not approve of the elaborate services and the finely decorated churches of the Benedictine monasteries; and they worked on the land with their own hands, cultivating their estates with the help of lay-brothers. They became some of the greatest raisers and owners of flocks of sheep in the country.

## Norman Cathedrals

While the monasteries were the centers of religious life, every village had its parish church, served by a parish priest; and these parishes, then as now, were organized in dioceses, each diocese being ruled over by a bishop, who had his throne in a great church or cathedral.

In Anglo-Saxon England there had been stone-built cathedrals often very large, sometimes standing, strangely enough, not in a big town but in a quite small country village. William the Conqueror brought to England a still more splendid tradition of cathedral building. The Anglo-Saxon cathedrals were pulled down by the Normans, and greater and finer cathedrals were built, always in a town of some size and importance.

The building of these great Norman cathedrals must have been a tremendous undertaking, for there was no question then of employing an architect who would obtain tenders from a firm of builders or contractors. The priests who were to serve the cathedral themselves bought all the materials, and engaged the masons, sculptors, craftsmen, and artists who were employed; it is remarkable how short a time it took to finish one of these huge buildings. Some cathedrals owned the lead mines and stone quarries from which their building materials came.

The Norman bishops were important members of the new feudal society in England, for they were also tenants-in-chief of the King — great landowners who were royal vassals and who often had the feudal responsibility of providing knights for the King's army. And, because they were far better-educated men than most of the other tenants-in-chief, bishops were frequently chosen as royal advisers. A few of these bishops were nothing more than bold bad barons in a thin clerical disguise — like Bishop Odo of Bayeux, the Conqueror's half-brother, who had fought at the battle of Hastings wearing armor and at the head of his one hundred and twenty knights. He had laid about him with a mace, because the Church of Rome disapproved of priests shedding blood with the sword.

Very often the parish church would be the only stone-built building in a village; and these churches, in a very real sense, were the centers of village life. Mass was said in them every day; the crude paintings on their whitewashed walls, showing the horrors of hell and the joys of Heaven, were the only pictures that a villager was ever likely to see; and at Christmas and at Easter and on the various Saints' Days the services and the processions that followed them were full of color and pageantry.

The parish priest, as a rule, belonged to the same class of men as the village farmers and, like them, he spent a great part of his working week cultivating his strips in the open fields. Although the Church of Rome did not allow its priests to marry, many village priests were either ignorant of this law or simply disregarded it, and were married men with families.

## The Crusaders

The Crusades are an example of the great influence that the Church possessed in a feudal society.

For centuries Christendom had been on the defensive, desperately trying to defend her frontiers against non-Christian invaders — the Hungarian Magyars, the Vikings, and the Saracens, or Arabs. Then, in due course, the Hungarians and the Vikings had been converted to the Christian faith; but the Saracens, who were of the Moslem faith but who were hated as much by the Christian Church as if they had been heathens, had captured Jerusalem and had occupied a great part of the country of Spain. By the year 1075 it had become impossible for Christian pilgrims to visit the Holy Places.

In 1095, feeling that the time had come for Christendom to turn and take the offensive, the Church preached the First Crusade, urging all the Kings and barons and knights in Western Europe to enlist in a Holy War to recapture Jerusalem and the lost Spanish territories.

The response to this appeal, and to the appeals for the later and less successful Crusades, was astonishing. Almost every nobleman in France took part, and although fewer English barons and knights fought under the banner of the Cross,

King Richard I played a notable part in the Third Crusade. The motives of the Crusaders were mixed. Some of them saw in these campaigns a practical way of serving God and of making certain that they would go to Heaven when they died. Others were attracted by an opportunity for fighting, for adventure, for seeing foreign lands, and for winning personal glory and obtaining rich booty and spoils.

## The Men Who Labored

Of all the classes of men in a feudal society, the men who labored were the most numerous, perhaps the least exciting, but, for all that, it may be thought, the most interesting.

After the Norman Conquest, all instead of some of the village farmers and the peasants in England had become "tenants" of the lords of the manors from whom they held the land which they cultivated; as was the case with all other feudal links, the links that bound lords of the manor with their free and their unfree tenants were partly personal and partly strictly practical.

A lord of a manor undertook to protect his tenant, to stand by him, if he was a free man, in the King's court of justice; to give him justice in his own manor court if he was unfree; and to provide him with "maintenance" in the shape of the strips in the open fields from the cultivation of which the tenant got his living.

A tenant, in his turn, had to swear an oath of fealty to his lord: "Hear this my Lord, I, Roger, [or whatever the tenant's name might be] will be faithful and loyal to thee, and faith to thee will bear of the tenement I hold of thee, and will be justiciable to thee in body and chattels. So help me God and the

Saints."

In addition to being loyal and faithful to his lord, a tenant, in return for the land he held, had to render his lord certain services.

The tenants of the lord of a manor who were free men, tenants, that is to say, who could prove that their fathers before them had been free men, had to pay their lord an annual rent for their land, sometimes in produce but more often in money; and, possibly to emphasize the personal nature of the link, they were also expected to give their lord presents — hens and loaves of bread at Christmas, and eggs at Easter, which is the origin of the custom of giving Easter Eggs. The lord, in his turn, was expected to give his free tenants a feast at Christmas time and at Easter.

### "Week Work" and "Boon Work"

The link between an unfree tenant or a villein, as he was called, and the lord of his manor, was rather different.

In the first place, a villein, who was regarded as unfree because his father before him had been unfree, was, in a sense, a "possession" of his lord. It was commonly said that he "owned nothing but his belly." He could not leave his manor and seek land and employment elsewhere without his lord's permission. And if a lord sold the land which an unfree tenant cultivated, the tenant and his wife and children could, in theory, be sold with it.

Then again, in return for their holdings of land, villeins were taxed each year by their lords, who could demand any sum that they chose, and they had to put in one, two, three, or even four days' work every week on their lords' domains — which might be either separate farms belonging to the manors, or strips scattered about in the open village fields. And, in addition to this regular year-in, year-out work, which was called "week work," they were also expected, out of the love that they were supposed to feel for their lords, to work extra time on the domains at especially busy times of the year such as haymaking and harvest. These extra services were called "boon work."

Free tenants as well as unfree tenants, and all the members of their families, were expected to perform boon work for their lords; and the lords, to show that they appreciated that this was a "voluntary" contribution to their well-being on the part of their tenants — although it was really a burden that no tenant could escape — generally provided the boon workers with their food and drink on boon days.

Villeins, as well as free tenants, were expected to give their lords the usual presents at Christmas and Easter; villeins were obliged to take their corn to be ground at their lords' mills — and to pay for this service; to make their bread in the lords' ovens; to fold their sheep on their lords' lands at certain times of the year — so that the lords' lands should be well-manured; and to pay their lords a sum of money when their daughters got married. They were even expected, when their lords were entertaining guests, to give up their blankets so that the guests would be warmly covered at night.

Added together, these sound like very heavy burdens — as indeed they were. For as much as half, or more than half, of his working life, a villein could not work on his own land, because he was obliged to work on his lord's domain. At the busiest times of his own farming year he had to leave his own haymaking and his own harvesting to help his lord get in his hay crop and his grain crops. But, in actual fact, the burdens may not have been quite as heavy as they sound. Villeins, if they had grown-up sons or unmarried brothers living in their houses, could send them to work on the lord's domain while they themselves cultivated their own strips; and some of the

richer villeins had farm servants of their own, who could do this work. The hours that a villein was expected to put in on his lord's land were not long, and "a day's work" on the domain only amounted, in practice, to half a day's work. And "boon work" seems generally to have been regarded as a social occasion when all the villagers got together and had a rather enjoyable time. The boon feasts were greatly looked forward to.

Nor was the villein quite as defenseless and helpless as it might appear. A lord depended on his villeins for the cultivation of his own domain; and it would not have been to his advantage to have treated these unfree tenants badly. A discontented villein could run away from his manor, and it might be difficult for a lord to find the runaway and to bring him back. If a villein escaped to a town, and managed to stay there for a year and a day, he was considered to be a free man. Then again, custom on the manors — the rule by which things had always been done — was very strong; and, on the whole, the new Norman lords were inclined to follow the old customs which had regulated the lives and work of the farmers before the Conquest.

## Life in a Medieval Village

The lives of these free and unfree tenants on a manor must have been rough and uncomfortable. The houses they lived in, set down on either side of the village street, were little better than wooden shacks, thatched with straw or reeds. A villager's house seldom had more than two rooms — a living-room and a small bedroom leading out of it. There were no chimneys, and no glass in the windows. But each house was

60

fronted by a garden, where vegetables and some flowers were carefully grown; and at the back there was a paddock, where a cow and a plow-oxen or two could graze, where fruit could be grown, and where hens and geese could scratch for a living. The food that the villagers ate was produced on their holdings of land. Their usual diet was flour — baked with peas and beans into bread, or boiled into puddings. Ale, which the men, women, and children all drank, was brewed from grain. Now and then a village household would kill and eat one of their tough razorback pigs; and on feast days and holidays a sheep might be slaughtered. Game could be speared or snared in the woods, but the notion was growing up that the woods, which had once belonged to the villages, were now the private properties of the lords of the manors. At this time the royal forests, in which no one but the King was allowed to hunt and in which game was strictly preserved, covered as much as one-third of the whole area of England.

Life must also have been hard for a villager's wife, who had to bring up her children, cook, and keep the house clean. Housewives were the only members of a tenant's family who were excused "boon work." One of the nicest things about the lives of these villagers is the affection that they felt for all the members of their families and the care and trouble that they took in looking after them. Even the old were not forgotten. When a father became too old or too crippled to look after his strips in the open fields, the son who took over from him often built another smaller house, or a single room, in the paddock of the family house, so that his parents would have somewhere of their own in which to end their days.

Another endearing thing is that all these villagers were called by their Christian names. Surnames did not come into use until after the year 1200. When they did, Dickson, Harrison, and Thompson were such common surnames that it seems likely that nicknames, such as Dick, Harry and Tom, must have been generally used. The usual way of giving a surname to someone was either to add "son" to his father's Christian name, or to call a man by the name of the place where he lived or by the name of his profession or calling — Barber, Smith, and so on. Barons were often given surnames by adding "Fitz" to the Christian names of their fathers — FitzStephen, for example.

## A Farmer's Year

The lives of these villagers were to a great extent governed by the season of the year, and followed a regular pattern.

Winter was thought of as lasting from Michaelmas September 29 until Christmas; and it was reckoned that the sowing of winter wheat and rye on all the strips in one of the two great "open" village fields that were being cultivated must be finished by All Hallows (November 1) or, at the latest, by Martinmas (November 11). On All Hallows Day, the cattle were driven in to the byres ("bowers") for the winter, and during the month of November such of the cattle and sheep as could not be kept through the winter through lack of foodstuff were slaughtered, and their meat salted down or dried. After the winter sowing was done came the plowing in preparation for the spring sowing and, that finished, the autumn's harvest was threshed in the barns with flails, and then winnowed to separate the grain from the chaff.

Spring lasted from Christmas until Holy Week; and the spring sowing of oats, barley, vetches, peas, and beans on all the strips in the second open field started on Candlemas Day (February 2), and had to be finished by Lady Day (March 25). On Candlemas Day the fences were put up round the hay-meadow, so as to prevent cattle eating the growing grass. The hay-meadow was then said to be "in defense."

Summer extended from Easter Day to Lammas Day (August 1). On May Day the cattle were taken out of the byres and turned out to pasture — sometimes they were so weak through lack of food that they had to be carried to the common; and in June the sheep were washed in streams or ponds, and then sheared. On Midsummer Day (June 24) hay-cutting began in the village hay-meadow. The hay crop had to be harvested by Lammas Day, when the movable fences round the hay-meadow were taken down, and the cattle were allowed in to graze.

Autumn was the period between Lammas Day and Michaelmas, and was sometimes called, appropriately, Harvest· Harvesting the grain crops began on Lammas Day, and had to be finished by Michaelmas Day. Michaelmas marked the end and

63

the beginning of the farmer's year. The harvest was in, and the fences that had been put up around the two fields under cultivation were taken down, and the cattle were allowed to feed on the stubbles.

## Saints' Days and Holidays

These Saint's Day landmarks were also kept as holidays.

On All Hallows Day, and especially on Halloween, witches might be seen; and this holiday was marked by the lighting of bonfires in honor, it was said, of the dead. The great holiday of the year for farmers was Christmas and its Twelve Days. Lords of the manor gave feasts to their tenants at Christmas; and the tenants themselves killed some of their sheep and pigs, and there was a vast amount of eating and drinking. January 7, the day after Epiphany, was called Plow Monday, when the young plowmen dragged their decorated plows up and down the village street. Shrove Tuesday was traditionally the day for sports and games in the villages.

Easter was the second great holiday of the year — and its holiday lasted until the second Monday after Easter Sunday, Hock Day. This was the occasion when lords of the manor gave another feast to their tenants. On May Day the village children picked branches of flowering hawthorn. The Gang Days — the Monday, Tuesday, and Wednesday before Ascension Day — were marked by beating the bounds of the parish, when small boys were bumped against tree stumps so as to make them remember these parish boundaries for the rest of their lives. Whitsunday was the next holiday; and then came Midsummer Day, the Feast of St. John. On Midsummer Day bonfires were always lit to drive away the dragons that were

supposed to be about. On Lammas Day loaves were made from that summer's corn, and were taken to the church to be blessed.

It will be noticed how closely tied up these holidays were with the festivals of the Church; and how pagan ideas and superstitions were confused with Church teaching and beliefs. Religion might have its frightening side for these villagers; but it had its colorful and exciting side as well.

In spite of the Norman Conquest, and in spite of the fact that the lords of the manors were generally French-speaking Normans, the tenants of the manors went on speaking Anglo-

Saxon, the language which developed into the English which is spoken and written today.

It is interesting to notice that whereas the names that are still used for animals — pigs, sheep, and bulls for instance — are Anglo-Saxon words, the words now used to describe the meat that comes from these animals — pork, mutton, and beef — are Norman-French in origin.

# Chapter 3
# The End

There was another class of people who played a considerable part in a feudal society — townspeople or, as they were called, burgesses.

In the feudal scheme of things, no difference was made between a town and a country village. In fact, in those days a village was generally called a "town" or a "township"; and an attempt was made to treat townspeople and villagers in exactly the same way.

This was obviously nonsense; and the reason that the attempt was made was because towns, and the up-and-coming and independently-minded people who lived in them, did not fit in with the feudal pattern.

The Romans, who were famous town-planners and town-builders, had planted cities all over Western Europe — walled towns with some substantial stone houses and magnificent public buildings. In England, even before the withdrawal of the legions, these Roman cities had been allowed to fall into decay; but some of them, Canterbury and Rochester, for instance, had been given a new importance because Kings or bishops had come to live in them, or because monasteries had been established in or near them. Later, some of these old Roman towns had been re-fortified by King Alfred as strongholds against the Viking invaders; and new walled towns, of which Oxford is an example, were built at strategic points and at river crossings.

Throughout all these troubled times London was the largest and most important town in England, and one of the most important cities in Western Europe.

## Why Towns Grew Up

As a rule, the business of buying and selling goods and making articles for sale was the main reason for a town's existence. Towns were places to which produce from the surrounding countryside — butter, eggs, meat, cheese, chickens, and so on — was brought to be sold, and where the villagers who sold these goods could buy other goods that they needed — salt, clothes, crockery, and iron for their agricultural implements. Salt, which was then in great demand, was carried all over England either in carts drawn by four or two horses, on packhorses, or by men with sacks on their backs.

On a much bigger scale, a great port like London was a place to which goods imported from abroad were sent, and from which exports from England were shipped overseas.

Kings, bishops, and monks were very good friends to towns. Produce from their widely scattered manors was regularly sent up to them from the country — it was one of the duties of the tenants of manors to act as carriers; and while most of the grain and meat and poultry and honey (which was then used in the place of sugar) was consumed by their enormous households, there was always some left over which was offered for sale in the towns at their gates. And they were also good customers for luxuries which could not be produced on their own estates. This encouraged traders in the towns to stock imported wine, muslins, spices of all kind (which disguised the nasty taste of half-rotten salted meat), and dried fruits and other luxury articles, because they knew that they would always have buyers for them. Craftsmen, too, were anxious to settle in towns, because there would be a demand for the articles that they made.

From the time of King Alfred onwards, the practice had grown up of offering building plots in town to people who might be tempted to take them up because of the attractive terms that they could obtain. A man could rent a site for a

house for a small annual money payment; and whereas a villager was not allowed to sell his house and his holding of land, a burgess, when he had built a house in town, could sell it whenever he liked; and, apart from his money rent, he owed no other services to his landlord.

For these reasons burgesses thought of themselves as being more "free" than villagers — which is why, after the Norman Conquest, villeins who ran away from their manors sought refuge in towns, where they were not always very welcome.

## Life in a Medieval Town

The Norman Conquest, at first, had a disastrous effect on English towns. In most towns either the King or the Norman baron to whom the King had granted the town built a castle, pulling down a good many of the burgesses' houses in the process; and the burgesses found, to their dismay, that the castle-builder generally tried to force them to undertake feudal services — ordering them, for example, to grind their corn only at his mill, to bake their bread only in his oven, and forbidding them to settle their disputes anywhere but in his own court, where the lord pocketed the fines that the people who had misbehaved were made to pay. William the Conqueror also granted a good many towns to bishops and abbots, and these churchmen proved to be the most unpopular landlords of all.

Nothing, however, could stop the growth of trade and commerce — England has always been called a nation of shopkeepers, and the towns began to flourish again. But the

burgesses, unlike the villagers, were impatient people. The feudal services demanded of them by the lords of their towns annoyed and angered them; they found that the delays in their lords' courts of law prevented them from getting on with their businesses. And so, having bought the privilege of holding weekly markets in their towns and of holding annual fairs which lasted for several days, the burgesses went on to purchase, either from the King or from the lords of their towns, what were called "Charters of Liberties." These Charters gave the burgesses the right to elect the members of their own town councils, freed them from feudal services, and allowed them to hold their own law courts, in which a special form of "trading law," which cut out unnecessary delays, was practiced. A Charter of Liberty also gave the burgesses the privilege of reaching an agreement on a lump-sum annual payment of the taxes and dues which they had to pay to the King. Without such an agreement they would have been at the mercy, each year, of the King's official, the sheriff, who would decide what they ought to pay.

The passion that burgesses had for managing their own affairs, free from outside interference, was also shown in the guilds that sprang up in most towns. These guilds were associations of traders and craftsmen. Dealers in different kinds of commodities and all the various craftsmen had their own guilds, which regulated the way in which their businesses and crafts were carried on. In any large town, the mayor, elected by the burgesses, was the principal officer of the town council, and among other duties was responsible for seeing that the shopkeepers of the town gave correct weights and measures, that too high prices were not asked for goods, that the ale sold was of the correct strength, and that the town was kept clean and well supplied with water. Aldermen were the representatives of

the various guilds on the town councils.

The houses that the burgesses lived in were generally made with wooden frameworks, filled in with dried mud mixed with straw; there are reported cases of thieves breaking into houses simply by knocking holes through their walls. Sometimes the houses of rich burgesses were made of stone. Houses in towns were taller than the houses in the villages, because their big living-rooms were generally on the second floors, the ground floors being used either as store-rooms or workshops. Passages running through these lower rooms led to enclosed yards at the back. Shops, were then usually stalls, like present-day market stalls, standing at the side of the road.

73

In France and in other Western European countries, where the burgesses formed what were known as "communes," the quarrels between the burgesses and the lords of their towns were much more bitter than they ever were in England. A "commune" came into being as the result of all the burgesses in a town taking a communal or joint oath to stand together to maintain and defend their rights and liberties.

Feudal barons were sometimes tempted to embark on what would now be thought of as speculative urban developments. The "new" town of Stratford-on-Avon was a case in point.

During the reign of Richard I (1189–99), John de Coutances, Bishop of Worcester, decided to establish a new market town on his country manor of Stratford; and he accordingly offered building plots on attractive terms to anyone who might want to take them up. By the year 1250 there were already two hundred and fifty householders in the new town; Stratford had a weekly market and three annual fairs; there was a trades-folk's guild with its own hospital, school, guildhall, and chapel; and, living in this thriving place, there were smiths, carpenters, wheelwrights, coopers (who made barrels), tilers, tanners, shoemakers, glovers, weavers, fullers, dyers, tailors, millers, bakers, cooks, butchers, mercers (who dealt in silk), a doctor, a piper, a woman minstrel, and several clergymen. William Shakespeare, many years later, was born in Stratford-on-Avon, the son of a glover.

London was the largest as well as the richest city in feudal England; and its burgesses, or citizens, were the most eager to obtain, and to defend, their liberties.

An excellent description of London as it was in the reign of King Henry II (1154–89) is given by William FitzStephen in his life of a famous Londoner, Thomas Becket.

FitzStephen writes of London's castles — the White Tower at its east end, and Baynard's Castle and Montfichet's Castle at its west end; of the great cathedral church of St. Paul's, and of the thirteen other great London churches and the hundred and twenty-six smaller ones; and of the royal palace of Westminster, two miles upstream from the city itself. He describes the London houses that belonged to the King's tenants-in-chief; the famous schools in which the monks taught; London's law courts; the houses outside the city, which were surrounded by gardens and trees; the fields where all kinds of games were played; and London's charities, London's elaborate water supply, and London's famous system of drainage. He even mentions a restaurant on the north bank of the river Thames where at any time of the day of night Londoners could obtain roast, fried, or boiled meat or, if they preferred it, fish, game, and poultry.

But he was evidently most impressed by London's fame as a "world's mart." He describes the communities of foreign traders, each of which had its own quarters in the town; and he writes of the great variety of goods that poured in to the city not only from the near and remote counties of England, but also from overseas.

Lead came from the mines in Yorkshire, Cumberland, and Derbyshire; iron from Sussex; tin from Cornwall; coal from

Newcastle; salt from Cheshire and elsewhere; meat, hides, bacon, and cheese from the home counties; and, above all, wool — from all over England. Vast amounts of English wool and woolen goods were shipped overseas every year from the port of London.

FitzStephen also describes the quantity and variety of the goods that arrived at the port of London from abroad — wine and dyes from France; fish, whale oil, pitch, tar, furs, and soft woods from Scandinavia; olive oil, soap, Cordova leather, figs, dates, almonds, sugar, oranges and lemons from Spain and Portugal; and all the luxuries of the East that were carried to London in Italian ships — silks, cloth-of-gold, currants, spices of all kinds, rubies and emeralds, sandalwood, cottons and muslins, and even monkeys and parrots.

## Changing Needs

Time and again, the study of history shows that arrangements that were made which may seem today to be quite extraordinary, were in fact sensible and practical, and the best arrangements that could have been made, *at that time*, to meet pressing and urgent needs.

Feudalism had met the needs of countries when war and violence were the rule rather than the exception, and when Kings were unable to protect their weaker subjects properly. Later, the feudal system had met the needs of Kings who required well-equipped and well-trained mounted soldiers for their armies. It also made certain that estates would be properly cultivated; and, at a time when coin of the realm was in short supply, it had made it possible for services of all kinds to be paid for by grants of land.

In Western Europe, by the year 1250, these particular needs no longer existed.

Peace and prosperity had become more usual than war and poverty. Because there were more well-educated men available to serve as royal officials and because roads were better and there were more bridges, Kings were able to govern more efficiently. Armies no longer depended to anything like the same extent on mounted barons and their knights. And, since coin of the realm was more plentiful, all classes of men, from the King downwards, had begun to discover that it was more convenient to pay people in cash, rather than in land, for the work that they did.

Under the feudal scheme of things, the King's tenants-in-chief, and their vassal knights, had undertaken to serve in the King's army for a period of only forty days in each year. This had been a reasonably suitable arrangement when wars had generally been short and local, and when fighting, as a rule, had stopped each autumn, to start up again, if necessary, in the following spring, although the feudal levies had never, probably, been adequate for the English Kings' purposes, and they had often been supplemented by paid foot-soldiers. By the year 1250, the wars that the Kings of England usually had to fight were campaigns in France, which lasted for much longer than forty days. Again, the mounted soldier was no longer the most important man in a battle. Archers, with their longbows, had come into their own; and companies of professional men-at-arms, mercenaries who would serve for any length of time for a daily money wage, were readily available.

## Cash Payments instead of Services

These changed circumstances had led the Kings of England, well before the year 1250, to make a new arrangement by which, instead of a baron himself serving with his knights in the King's army, he was allowed to pay the King an annual

sum in money, known as "scutage."

It would be a mistake to imagine that scutage was simply an ingenious device invented by the English Kings in order to weaken the power of the barons. The barons also found that scutage was convenient. Providing the full number of properly trained and properly armed knights for the King's army had never been easy. It had been a fairly simple matter when knights had lived in their lord's houses; it had become much more difficult after the custom had grown up of providing knights with their own estates; and matters had become still more difficult when it had become customary that a knight's son, on the payment of a sum of money, could inherit the family estate, or fee, on his father's death. The son of a man who had been a first-rate mounted soldier might prove to be a far less efficient warrior than his father; the heir of a knight might sometimes be his daughter, who would then herself have to find and provide a knight for the army; and sometimes a single knight's fee had been split up into halves, quarters, or even tenths, so that it would be the responsibility of two, or four, or as many as ten people to provide one knight. Furthermore, the money that the barons had to find in order to pay the King scutage did not come out of their own pockets. The money was found by their knights who, in their turn, got at least some of it from the tenants of their manors.

Bishops and abbots had always found it difficult to provide the knights that the King required from them. At first, in many monasteries, these soldiers had lived with the monks, but their noisy behavior had proved distracting to the peaceful, well-ordered life of a monastery. So these knights, too, had been given fees of their own; but there had been endless complaints that when they served with the King's army they were neither properly armed nor sufficiently well-trained.

There was another reason why the payment of scutage was welcomed by the King's tenants-in-chief. By the year 1250, many of the barons, though they were still fighting men at heart, no longer regarded fighting on horseback as the be-all and end-all of their existences. They now had other interests, including the profitable development of their estates. More land was being put under cultivation; more crops were being grown for sale and not simply for consumption by their growers; new towns were being started; and great sheep runs were being planned to meet the growing demand for wool. In 1066 feudal barons would have been ashamed of being interested in such matters. Two hundred years later they had become very interested indeed.

Many knights, too, must have welcomed the introduction of scutage. Some of them, living quietly on their estates, had become, over the years, what would today be called "country gentlemen," interesting themselves in the farming of the domains of their manors, and taking their part, on the King's orders, in the legal business of the shires, or counties, in which they lived. Others, having enthusiastically adopted the new fashion of "chivalry" introduced from France, either sought adventure as knights-errant by hiring themselves out, with companies of men-at-arms, to the highest bidder, or amused themselves and gained a living by going around from tournament to tournament, winning prizes and claiming ransoms from the knights whom they managed to defeat in the lists.

## The Rules of Chivalry

Chivalry was a very strange business. Originally, a knight was simply a professional soldier who had been trained to fight on horseback; and a youth, after completing his training, had been "dubbed" knight in a rough-and-ready ceremony.

Then in France, Germany and Italy — and to a lesser extent in England — the custom had grown that before this ceremony the knight-to-be should lay his sword for a moment on the altar of a church. Later, it had become the custom for the ceremony of dubbing a knight to be performed not by an older knight but by a bishop. The bishop would bless each piece of equipment before he handed it to the new knight, and he "dubbed" the knight by touching the youth's neck with his sword before he fastened it round his waist. Only the new knight's spurs

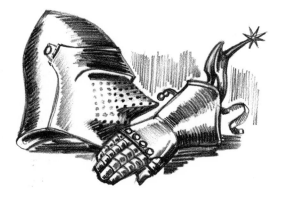

were always handed to him by a layman. Before the ceremony, the knight-to-be would be expected to recite the rules of chivalry, and to swear a sacred oath that he would be true to them all his life; and occasionally he was expected to spend the night before the ceremony in a vigil of prayer.

The rules of chivalry were very strict. A knight was expected to be generous; he must pursue glory; he must disregard pain, fatigue, and death; his sword must be used only in good causes, especially to defend the Holy Church against the infidel; he must protect widows, orphans, and the poor; and he must help

81

all fellow-beings in distress.

A prayer, carved in the stone of the porch of Chartres cathedral in France, expresses the spirit of these rules:

Most Holy Lord, Almighty Father . . . thou who hast permitted on earth the use of the sword to repress the malice of the wicked and defend justice; who for the protection of thy people hast thought fit to institute the order of chivalry . . . cause thy servant here before thee, by disposing his heart to goodness, never to use this sword or another to injure anyone unjustly; but let him use it always to defend the Just and Right.

This new fashion — for that, in a sense, was what chivalry really was — changed the ways in which knights were regarded by other people. Before, they had simply been tough rank-and-file fighting soldiers. As a result of the introduction of chivalry, knights were looked on, especially in France, Germany, and Italy, as a class of men apart, dedicated to the service of God in arms; and if knightly vows were not always faithfully observed by all knights and the vigils of prayer were simetimes enlivened by music and dancing, chivalry nevertheless changed the manners and outlooks of knights in many important ways.

## A New Deal for Ladies

A knight was expected to treat all ladies with great respect; each bachelor knight was expected to choose a lady of noble birth, older than himself, for whom he was to have feelings of what was called "courtly love"; and he was expected to appreciate poetry, music, and the arts. All the present-day romantic notions about knights come from this fashion of chivalry; and the idea of the "chivalrous" treatment of women dates from this time. Women, of course, benefited from this new attitude. They felt themselves to be more important; they were listened

to by men when they talked about and became interested in other things than their children and their household duties; and, as a sign of the new confidence that they felt, their clothes became more elaborate, with long sleeves trailing to the ground.

Tournaments, too — which, with hunting, were the chief recreations of knights and for some of them a source of livelihood — underwent a complete change. Mêlées, or mock battles, went out of fashion; and jousts, or single-combats between two knights fighting with blunted weapons, took their place. Later, barriers were put up in the "lists," as the tournament grounds were called, so as to prevent the jousters' horses colliding with one another; very strict rules were laid down. Tournaments, instead of being grim and dangerous rehearsals for actual warfare, became popular fêtes or entertainments. Kings and barons, as well as knights, took part in them; jousters wore the

new elaborate plate armor that had taken the place of the old mail shirts, and the new huge "pot" helmets that had ousted the old conical helmets; heraldry, which was another new fashion, added color and romance to the scene, for the jousters displayed their crests and devices on their helmets and shields, on the surcoats that they wore over their armor, and on the trappers, or skirts, of their horses; heralds acted as the masters of ceremonies; and ladies often acted as the judges of these encounters, and presented the prizes to their winners.

In France, Germany, and Italy, knights were regarded as noblemen; and as a rule only the sons of knights could be dubbed knights. This never happened in England. English knights became a part of the great middle class of men; any fairly rich man, whatever his father had been, could be made a knight. Only the King's tenants-in-chief came to be regarded as hereditary peers of the realm.

Scutage was not the only money payment that, by the year 1250, was being regularly paid in the place of personal services.

Knights were excused garrison duties in their barons' castles in return for paying an annual money sum, which made it possible for their lords to pay men-at-arms and sergeants to guard their castles, which, by this time, were beginning to resemble the medieval castles of popular imagination, with high stone keeps towering above baileys which, in their turn, were defended by strong stone walls, towers, and moats filled with water.

Hardly any of the holders of estates originally granted to their fathers, grandfathers, or great-grandfathers in return for the domestic and personal services that they had rendered to the King or to his tenants-in-chief were still performing these services. The descendants of a royal cook, for example, had probably become a country gentleman who paid someone else

to cook in the royal palace.

And even on the manors, where change came more slowly, a few villeins had begun to pay their lords annual rents in money in order to be excused from working on their domains; and the lords of the manors, with these rents in their pockets, were able to pay day-laborers a money wage.

## Magna Carta

Because the particular needs that the feudal system had met had to a great extent disappeared, most feudal arrangements, by the year 1250, had either been dropped or had become twisted and distorted.

Originally, the feudal links between different classes of men had been very personal links, in which "aid and friendship" had played an important part. The vassal not only had to render services to his lord, he was also his lord's faithful friend; and the lord pledged himself to protect and befriend "his man." The lord of a manor was not merely the landlord of his tenants; he was also supposed to be their friend and their protector, and the tenants had to promise to be faithful to and respect their lord.

How the personal side of these links had almost entirely disappeared on the manors has already been described; and by the year 1250 something of the same kind had happened to the links between a vassal and his lord.

Many of the quarrels between the Kings of England and their feudal tenants-in-chief — including the quarrels that led up to the signing of Magna Carta in the year 1215 — concerned the King's right, by feudal custom, to look after his vassal's heirs if these heirs inherited their fathers' estates before they were old enough to look after them, and his right to find suitable husbands for the widows and heiresses of his vassals.

These rights had been, at first, duties owed to his vassals by the King in the way of friendship. A vassal died, and it was the King's duty to befriend the dead man's widow, his young son, and his daughters. In course of time these responsibilities had been turned by the King, and by his tenants-in-chief in their dealings with *their* vassals, into sordid means of making money. The King or one of his tenants-in-chief would seize the estate of a vassal who had not yet come of age, and would sell the right to enjoy the income from it to the highest bidder; and in the same way widows and heiresses of vassals were heartlessly sold in marriage to whoever would pay the highest prices.

What new needs had arisen by the year 1250, and what were the new arrangements which could best meet them?

A short answer, so far as England was concerned, would be to say that the main needs were for the complete supremacy throughout the country of a uniform system of royal justice that was fair, available to everyone, and free from the interference of individual nobles, who were anxious to keep their own private courts of law because they pocketed the fines that were imposed in them; and for the establishment of a system of the government in which the "new men" in the Kingdom, the knights of the shires and the burgesses of the towns, who were now ready to assume responsibilities, should have a share with the great tenants-in-chief in saying how the country should be governed.

The most important of the arrangements that grew up to meet these new needs were the Common Law and Parliament.


## The Beginnings of Parliament

Both the Common Law and Parliament grew from the feudal right of tenants-in-chief to "advise" the King.

Assembled in the King's Great Council, these nobles, the barons and the bishops and the abbots, offered advice not only on important matters of state but also on such personal questions as to whether the King should marry. As was only natural, some of the tenants-in-chief attended the meetings of the Great Council very seldom; and of those who attended oftener, only a few were sufficiently well-educated and well-informed to give the King useful advice. In course of time, these few trusted advisers had formed small committees, each committee specializing in one particular subject.

One committee had specialized in the business of how taxes could best be collected; and its members had been given the name of the Barons of the Exchequer. Another committee had specialized in law. Its members were known as the Royal Justices, and they had hammered out a new system of law — the Common Law of England — which gradually took the place of the various customs which made up the law by which cases up to this time had been settled both in the royal courts, and in the private feudal courts, up and down the country.

The next step had been for members of the Great Council, which still survives in England today in the shape of the House of Lords, to act not as individual advisers but as a body, making demands from the King that were, at first, selfish demands that would benefit only themselves. Next, by reason of their growing influence and importance, knights of the shires and burgesses from the towns were sometimes summoned to attend the Great Council. The final step towards the establishment of Parliament was the demand that the imposing of new taxes should not be made without the consent, in Parliament, of the representatives of the people who would have to pay them. At first, the knights and burgesses, "the Commons," who were summoned to attend meetings of the Great Council, tried to avoid this expensive duty. Later, these representatives would actually be elected by the votes of the people whom they represented, and it would be considered a great honor to be a member of the House of Commons.

It was no small achievement that the feudal system had prevented Kings from becoming all-powerful dictators and great nobles from becoming local despots. And in a general way feudalism had also accomplished something else of importance.

Feudalism, by dividing society into those who worked and those who received the wealth produced by the workers — which sounds a most unfair arrangement — had made certain that most of the small amount of money that was then available passed into the hands of a very few men.

This again sounds unfair, but in a society in which everyone has to work very hard, and in which everyone is poor, and in which no one has any leisure, it would be impossible for great cathedrals to be built, or for books to be written, or for the people who import or make and sell luxury goods to find any buyers for them.

The feudal system gave England Canterbury and Salisbury and Winchester and all its other magnificent cathedrals; it gave France its great cathedrals like Chartres and Rheims; it allowed monks to copy existing books and to write their histories; and it encouraged the growth of London and of all the other great trading ports and cities in Western Europe.


## The End of the Feudal System

Of course, even after the need for them had gone, all the feudal links and arrangements did not disappear in a single night, or even in a hundred years.

Barons and knights went on fighting on horseback wearing plate armor that grew heavier and more elaborate until first the supremacy of the archer, and then the invention and the general use of gunpowder, made these top-heavy warriors and their "impregnable" castles useless and ridiculous.

The tenants of country manors continued for a long time to be linked to their lords by feudal ties, and to cultivate their

91

strips in the open fields in the same old way, but by the year 1600 there was not a single unfree villein left in England. In France, however, these feudal links between peasants and their lords lasted on until the French Revolution in 1789.

Estates continued to be held in England in return for feudal services for nearly three hundred years after 1250, although these services had become a mere farce. In France and Germany, once again, military service in return for the holding of land lasted much longer; and on several occasions King Louis XIV (1642–1715) called upon all his feudal vassals to serve in his army.

Some faint echoes of feudalism can still be heard today. If the government of a country or the way in which a business is run is described as being "feudal," it suggests that it is old-fashioned, and that too much power is held by the men at the top, and too little power enjoyed by the people at the bottom. Feudalism has become a term of reproach. But professional soldiers are still admired and respected. People are still said to treat other people "in a chivalrous way." And it is greatly to be hoped that what was best in the spirit of the feudal "oaths of fealty" will never quite disappear in present-day societies.

# Index

94

Montfichet's Castle, 75
Morrow Mass, 49
motte-and-bailey castles, 44

"nasal," 17
Norman cathedrals, 53-54
Norman conquest, 32, 33, 36, 38-39, 42-44, 56, 60, 65, 69, 71
Northmen, 33

Oath of Fealty, 14-15, 16, 19, 20, 38, 39, 56-57; and churchmen, 21; and peasant serfs, 21-22
Odo, of Bayeux, Bishop, 54
open-field farming, 35-36
Oxford, 68

Parliament, 89-90
peasant-serf, *passim*; 12, 14, 20, 21-22, 37, 43; life of, 56-64
Plow Monday, 64
Pope, 48
Prime, service of, 49
property in feudalism, 20-22, 39, 41

quintain, 26

religion under feudalism, 39, 45-56, 64-66
Richard I, 56, 74
Rochester, 67
Roman Empire, 10, 67-68

St. Paul's Cathedral, 75

Saints' Days, 64-65
Saracens, 19, 55
scutage, 78-80, 86
serf, *see* peasant-serf
sergeants, 41
Shakespeare, William, 74
Shrove Tuesday, 64
slaves, 12, 37
squire, 26
steward, 23
stirrups, 17
Stratford-on-Avon, 74
surnames, 62

tenant, life of, 56-64
thanes, 36-39, 43
Tierce, service of, 49
tournaments, 23, 85-86
towns, rise of and life in, 67-74; *see also* London
trading law, 72

vassal, *passim*; 14-16, 19, 20, 38, 41
Vespers, 51
Vikings, 19, 33, 37, 55, 68
villeins, 58-60, 87, 92

water-clocks, 32
week work, 58-60
Westminster palace, 75
White Tower, 75
Whitsunday, 64
William the Conqueror (Duke William of Normandy), 32, 33, 38-39, 41, 42, 44, 48, 53, 54, 71

# The Author

Thirty-six years ago, when he was working against the clock for his final examinations at Oxford, Ralph Arnold promised himself that one day, when he had sufficient leisure time, he would devote himself to the study of history at his own pace and in his own way.

The opportunity came when he retired from the chairmanship of a well-known firm of London publishers. Now he lives in the country, surrounded by a large number of books, "delighted," he says, in Bede's words, "to learn, or teach or write."

The teaching and writing parts of Mr. Arnold's new way of life have taken the shape of trying to write the kind of history books for children that he himself would have enjoyed when he was young. *Kings, Bishops, Knights and Pawns* is the first.